LET IT BE

SPEAKING WORDS
OF WISDOM…
SORT OF

By:

Max M. Power

© 2016 Cover by Pictures On The Go

Writing With Power
Let It Be
Second Edition

Printed in the United States of America

DEDICATION

For Veronica and Gabrielle.

Thank you for believing I could become a writer.

I would like to say a special thank you to all women in the world. You have a stronger influence in the world, more than you will ever know. Even if we do not show it at times, men would be lost without the women in our lives.

I have had the good fortune to have been influenced by very strong women. From my grandmother who taught me that a lack of funds did not mean I could not live a rich and fulfilling life, to my many aunts who would slap me around, reminding me how good I had it while their own children did not.

From my mother who always rode my ass, remaining tough and strict, despite her feelings of wanting to give in, making sure I walked a path of light instead of slipping into an abyss of darkness forever, to my sisters who would pick fights with me for no other reason than they could because they are my sisters and it's their job to torment me as such. To my dying day I know one of my sisters will still make me scream in frustration and smile, that's what siblings do.

From the many teachers who put up with the headache that was me as a student, desperately trying to teach me something to the one teacher who planted the seed that grew into my path that is writing. Thank you Mrs. Williams.

From my wife who gave me the greatest gift of all, our daughter, another strong woman that will drive me crazy because that is her role as a daughter. Everything I do I do for my family, to provide a better life than I have.

From my many friends who read what I write and demand I give them more, to those that threaten I would regret it if I ever stopped writing.

To Tyra Banks, whom I have never met, but with one single general question to the world, unlocked the flood gates that allows me to write so freely.

To the many future women I will meet in my life and in one way, shape, or form will inspire me to write something.

Even the bible acknowledges women as a great army. They certainly are the backbone of my life and for that I wish to say, "THANK YOU!!!"

I would like to thank the members of my fan club. For pushing me to be a better writer than I thought I could be. For always demanding more of me and never accepting NO for answer, this book is for you. As always:

"Submitted for your approval…"

This book is unique in the sense that it is comprised strictly of memes. These are thoughts that I had while I was battling my afflictions of anxiety, bipolar, and depression. Putting my thoughts down on paper helps me to get through my struggles. My hope is that these memes will help you too.

If you have not done so I would suggest you read *Lost Inside*, my first book on the subject of Mental Issues. It has helped people to be able to express themselves to those who do not have any afflictions to better understand what we go through.

Since writing *Lost Inside* I have begun taking classes in psychology, in hopes of better understanding what I am going through, and to better understand and help those around me who find themselves without a voice to express their inner demons. It is a long road I have chosen to travel down but those that I have helped, so far, along the way and those I know I will help in the future make this journey worth it.

We are all drowning in a sea of emotions and no matter how strong of a swimmer we are, we all need a life preserver to help keep us afloat. It is okay to ask for help. You are never alone, you do not have to weather your storms alone. Help is here. I am here. You have but only to ask.

I hope you enjoy this book and share it others who need it as well.

I would like this book to go hand and hand with *Lost Inside*.

The following introductions are from *Lost Inside*.

From *Lost Inside*:
Introduction

First off let me start this book with a disclaimer. I do **NOT**, have a degree in anything, least of all psychology, but then again, I really don't believe in most that do.

I say this because I've been challenged in the past about what gives me the right to give advice to people with depression, bipolar, or other mental issues. That my advice is dangerous to them because I am not a psychologist.

Well, what gives you the right? Just because you have a piece of paper that gives you a title? Now I said MOST earlier because when speaking with those who have challenged me I ask, "Do you have depression, bipolar, or any other mental issues you treat?" Usually the answer is, "No."

You use phrases like, *I understand, I know what you're going through,* and *I see* but in actuality you do not. How can you "understand" how I'm feeling if you've never felt it before? How can you "know what I'm going through," if you yourself have never been through it? How can you "see" what I'm talking about if you've never experienced it? Simply put, you can't! You can *guess* at it, but you will never know.

But you think you know better than me because you have a degree and I don't. Well all I can say to that is, would you mind if I wipe my ass with that piece of paper, cause to me that's all it's worth.

With that stated, all I have left to offer those who have these mental issues is my voice. I can only speak to what I feel and what I have been through. If you feel the same, have experienced what I have experienced, then by all means share my words. I know the hardest thing to do is express how you feel to someone who has no idea how you feel. My goal is to build a bridge between those two worlds and offer understanding to those who truly do not understand.

The following are things I have written when I have hit rock bottom. These things remind me that I come from a bad place in my past and I escaped it. I survived.

These short stories and poems remind me of where I have been and where I need to go. While I may visit these bad memories I do not let them consume me.

These are my emotions, my experiences, my joys, my pains, my own words. I hope you find them helpful.

I also hope by sharing my pain you will be inspired to share your pain with others. I hope to have touched your life as you have touched mine. Though we may have never met, your pain is my pain. We are bonded together forever by our will to survive.

I would like to know what you think of this book. If you wish to send a copy of this book to someone free of charge let me know. All comments are welcomed. It's cool if you don't respond but please pass this on to others. Don't let the chain end with you!

Sincerely,

Max M. Power

NOT a psychologist

Ask Yourself

For the lack of a better term I am using "Mental Issue," M.I. for short, as a blanket term to describe what we have and deal with on a daily basis. I want to use "Issue" because I don't want to call it an "Illness." Illness, to me anyway, implies that it can be cured, it's something that you caught and didn't have before. It's a part of us, it's in our DNA, it's something we didn't choose to have but something we live with on a daily basis.

When our M.I. kicks in it's called "An Episode." An Episode of what? Are we a sitcom or drama that people sit back and watch? While it may certainly feel this way for non M.I.s, for those of us going through said "episode" it feels more like a storm. Comes on with little to no warning. A lot of huffing and puffing, with loud crashes of thunder. For this reason I will refer to them as Storms and not "Episodes."

The following questions I came up with to help those non M.I.s start a discussion with those with M.I.s. By talking we can begin healing and understanding on both sides. Ask these questions and listen to the answers, don't judge, don't speak, just listen.

Questions:

1. What type of M.I. do you have?

2. When did you first suspect you might have this?

3. How did you feel before you found out and now that you know?

4. Do you take medication for your M.I.?

5. How do you deal with your M.I. on a daily basis?

6. Do you have any triggers for your storms, like a certain movie, song, or date?

7. How do you know a M.I. Storm is coming and how do you feel when it hits you?

8. What do you do to weather the Storm?

9. What's your biggest fear with regards to your M.I.?

10. Can you share an example of living with your M.I.?

11. What advice would you give to others who suspect they might have what you have?

Author's Note

This book is dedicated to those poor souls who feel lost inside themselves. Depression is a powerful enemy to overcome. It is something that attacks without remorse and pounds on our very being until we succumb to its will. At times we may feel helpless in our fight against depression but I am here to say that our battle is not without victory.

Some bouts with depression are brought on by a sad event in our lives. The loss of a loved one, a bad break-up, hurtful words thrown our way. Then there are times when depression attacks without reason. No matter what the cause, each of us will deal with depression in different ways.

There are those who may be able to brush away depression as easily as brushing away cob webs from their face. For those select few I say, consider yourselves fortunate. There are those who suffer greatly.

Their pain is so great that they feel alone in the world. Inside a large crowd they are the only ones around for miles. They are saddened by this great void which causes them to become invisible. While many may feel this way I can say with the utmost certainty that you are not alone. There are those who have felt your pain.

While this pain, this hurt, this ultimate suffering, continues to grow it needs an outlet of escape. Some turn to drinking to numb the pain, in hopes it will go away. Others turn to drugs, attempting to destroy the very vessel that depression inhabits. There are those who eat, disgusted by the monster they feel consuming them. Still others cut themselves, hoping the pain will escape through their open wounds.

But there is another avenue of escape that has crossed the minds of millions around the world. Suicide. Death is the ultimate escape, promising that you will feel no more pain. It calls to us, beckoning us to a peaceful being. It seems like a logical escape but nothing could be further from the truth.

While you may feel alone and that no one cares about you I say again you are wrong.

You have touched lives in ways you may never know but once your flame has burned out there will be those that will mourn your passing. Depression will have won and started its vicious cycle over again.

By the mere fact that you are reading these words is proof that someone cares. I care. I care enough to share my feelings with you. As you read this book there is no one else in the world but you and I. As you finish you will begin to see others who care about you also.

If someone has given you this book then there is another person who cares about you. If you care about someone else please pass this book on to them. Together we can build a chain of love one person at a time. Husbands and wives, mothers and fathers, daughters and sons, teachers and students, perfect strangers. We all have one thing in common: The Human Spirit, which is unbreakable if we allow others to care for us. Together we can defeat depression. Together we can survive.

Max   M.   Power

Let It Be

Speaking words of wisdom…
sort of

An Open Letter to Caregivers:

For you caregivers out there, when you find yourselves frustrated and saying, "I don't understand. I don't know how to help you," just remember, for those of us living with depression, neither do we.

While there are deeper emotions and darker demons I am fighting, my own personal monster as it were, what I am about to describe is a generic base of how most people with depression feel. Take from it what you will.

What must be understood, is that what goes up must come down and that includes us. It's nothing you or I did, it just is.

One day while I was driving home from work I was on a high, happy, singing in my vehicle at the top of my lungs like Tom Cruise in Jerry Maguire. It's ironic that the song he was singing is titled *Free Falling* because that's what happened next.

A car pulled up next to me at a red light,

close to my home. The woman was wearing a gallon of perfume because the smell drifted in the rain soaked air toward me.

BOOM!

Without warning a memory triggered, then another, then another. The next thing I knew I came crashing down to Earth, with no way to brace myself.

In the span of a literal second I managed to not only crash but to bury deep underground, the impact causing my world to collapse around me.

I couldn't see, my eyes were liquefied with tears.

I couldn't breathe, the air being sucked out of my body as I began to ache all over.

The pain became so great that as the light changed I had to pull over to the side of the road and park.

The monster deep inside began to crawl out, saying the key words that weaken me and makes it easier for it to take over.

"You're the true monster. You're worthless. You're not good enough." And the ever glass shattering, "No one loves you."

Thoughts of ending it all did cross my mind

but those were just that, thoughts, and not actions. I've learned long ago that I am not strong enough to follow through with those actions. I will always cower out.

Make no mistake, it takes true strength to follow through. For you caregivers, be thankful if your love one is too weak not to complete the act, if they were not they would be gone.

I made the effort to slowly make it home. Inside I was still dying and there was nothing anyone could do about it. I just have to wait for my storm to pass.

So don't give up on us, caregivers, for we are all weathering this storm together.

To My Younger Self:

Growing up in the 80's if you had a problem you were expected to keep it to yourself. You could either solve it on your own or burry that shit deep inside where it could never see the light of day. After all, it was your problem, or a family problem, and the outside world did *not* need to know about it. Therapy was for the rich, and for a poor person like me, I was shit out of luck.

My depression manifested itself at a very early age. I was in kindergarten when the darkness found me, wrapped me in its arms, and claimed me for itself. I did not know why I felt the way I felt, I just knew I didn't like it. I did try to ask for help and was denied. That's just the way things were back then, completely different from the way things are today.

I had to learn to live with my depression. I had to learn how to hide it and hide it well. And hide it I did. As the years went by my fear of being discovered grew into anxiety. I did not want to be locked away in some room somewhere, never to see my family ever again. These were the things a child thought would happen, and I carried that fear with me into adulthood, until one day, that fear became a reality.

We need to end the stigma of what people think these afflictions are and replace them with the reality of the effect they have on us. That fear of being discovered still exist, in myself and in countless others as well.

Often I am asked, if I want to change the narrative, what would I tell my younger self? I would say:

You have experienced great pain at an early age and as much as you want it to go away, it won't. You will want to end it but you are too weak to end it yourself. Oh how you will suffer from your pain and no one will ever know, for you hide it well.

You will endure the pain and use it to build strength. You will become a warrior because a younger version of yourself is going to need that strength to endure their own pain.

You know who you are and what the monster within is capable of. You know you are cursed but knowing allows you to fight. Fight on little warrior, your future depends on it.

To know you truly are worthless
speaks volumes.
Actions are all the proof you need.

Max M. Power

No matter what I do I'm always the bad guy. Time to embrace it!

Max M. Power

When my beast is released,
You will suffer,
Until it can be tamed,
Once again.

Max M. Power

I am so tired of being alone.

Max M. Power

When you're always strong sooner or later you break.

Max M. Power

Why am I so... worthless?

Max M. Power

When someone calls you crazy, you just answer, "Batshit certified!"

Max M. Power

What do you do when your child suffers because of you, where they live in pain, torment that drives them insane?

Max M. Power

Those that crave love the most always end up lonely.

Max M. Power

The ugliest creatures are
often the most gentle.

Max M. Power

To know your true worth,
or rather,
worthlessness,
is truly a blessing,
or rather,
a curse.

Max M. Power

*I know the darkness well.
She engulfs me and
embraces me like no other.
We are one, the darkness
and I.*

Max M. Power

No matter what the day
brings, remember to smile
and it will be a better day
because your smile is now
a part of the universe.

Max M. Power

Sometimes there isn't enough light in the world to drown out the darkness within.

Max M. Power

Alone
I'm
drowning.

Max M. Power

*I'm not afraid of dying.
I'm afraid of dying while
I'm alone.*

Max M. Power

Her eyes became the death of me, for when I looked into them I fell into a love that can never be.

Max M. Power

Everyday it gets harder to
fake a smile.

Max M. Power

Sometimes you just have to
accept your fate and play
until the bitter end.

Max M. Power

When your soul is on fire you need a team to help calm the flames. Asking for help is okay.

Max M. Power

*I begin to freeze as my soul
is wrapped up in a blanket
of darkness.*

Max M. Power

My demons three
Have beaten me down,
Making sure my smile
Is a permanent frown.

Max M. Power

*There comes a time
when you just want to
shout,
"Fuck it, I'm done."*

Max M. Power

*Sometimes I
really hate
this fucking world.*

Max M. Power

I want to be touched, to be held, to be told I am not the monster I've been told I am my entire life.

Max M. Power

When I walk through the gates of
hell I'm going to say,
"Luci, I'm home!"
The devil will run and hide. Then
I will know where I truly belong.

Max M. Power

Be the type of leader
that you wish to follow.

Max M. Power

When you're drowning inside asking for help is okay.

Max M. Power

*I'm not afraid of Death...
it's living that scares the
shit out of me.*

Max M. Power

I never chose to be lonely...
and yet,
here I am.

Max M. Power

You are mine.
My pain is yours.
You shall fulfill
my darkest desires.

Max M. Power

When I look in the mirror all that I see is the devil staring back at me.

Max M. Power

I've had my moments...
but they are all gone now.

Max M. Power

*A monster cares not for
the lives he destroys.
Their souls I will devour.
I am a monster, a very bad
boy.*

Max M. Power

Music is life.
It changes with your
emotions.

Max M. Power

One day my world will go dark and then... nothing.

Max M. Power

Just because you can't see them doesn't mean my demons do not exist.

Max M. Power

My eyes seen you
My heart loved you
My soul touched you
My memory will never
forget you.

Max M. Power

*What is more selfish, me
wanting to end my pain
forever or you keeping me
in pain to avoid your
own?*

Max M. Power

*I am
the devil
you refuse
to see.*

Max M. Power

Alone,
with my thoughts,
is the scariest place
on Earth.

Max M. Power

In a sea of voices I cry out. Silence is all that can be heard.

Max M. Power

All I want when my demons attack is for someone to take me in their arms, look me in my tear filled eyes and whisper, "This too shall pass."

Max M. Power

Silence

can

destroy

a soul.

Max M. Power

*I never wish to be alone
and yet solitude is thrust
upon me.*

Max M. Power

Inside I'm screaming,
But only silence remains.
Nothing can escape,
My soul is insane.

Max M. Power

There is only so much space you can give a person before you yourself fall off of the cliff.

Max M. Power

*I would rather be
bombarded by stones than
by words.
Stones hurt less.*

Max M. Power

I am not the Superman

you think I am.

Max M. Power

An amazing view can make you feel on top of the world or make you feel completely alone.

Max M. Power

Sometimes I just want to be held.

Max M. Power

You can be in heaven but a deafening whisper can bury you in the darkest corners of hell.

Max M. Power

I can hear them whispering,
My demons three.
They are saying,
What is soon to be.

Max M. Power

*If you hold no worth to the
one you want to be worth
something to, does that not
indeed make you
worthless?*

Max M. Power

Worthless, Ugly, Stupid,
Loser, Phony, Weak,
monster, Monster,
MONSTER!
These are words
I hear in my head.

Nobody loves you,
You're not good
enough,
Just end it all.
These are why,
I wish I was dead.

Max M. Power

The most horrific person I know is staring back at me in the mirror.

Max M. Power

"I'm here for you,"
means we talk on my terms,
not yours.

Max M. Power

Telling someone,
"I love you,"
does not mean you get to
control their life.

Max M. Power

When someone says,
"I want to die,"
the conversation should be
about their "Why," not about
why you think they are wrong.

Max M. Power

You may not be
perfect
but your soul
is perfect for me.

Max M. Power

Tight

When I hug you tight,
My soul is actually crying.
Life is dragging me under,
No matter how hard I'm trying.

Darkness surrounds me,
Deeper into the abyss I fall.
That's why I hug you tight,
I'm trying not to end it all.

Max M. Power

What would happen,
If I just faded away,
Consumed by the black hole,
That is my depression?

Would anyone notice,
Would anyone care,
About my bipolar, anxiety,
And many other afflictions?

Can I escape,
The vast emptiness inside?
Let's find out,
As my soul fades away.

Max M. Power

Trust should not be
easily gained
but earned,
for when it is
it's well worth it.

Max M. Power

Sometimes your
mind is your worst
adversary.

Max M. Power

I have mental afflictions yet silent I remain. My silence is manifested by one simple truth, FEAR!
Fear I will be judged. Fear I will be treated differently. Fear I will be locked up once more. These fears are very real. They have happened before. Only by ending the stigma of mental afflictions can I be free to express myself.

Max M. Power

Sanity is nothing more than an illusion.

Max M. Power

You have the power to destroy me and you don't even know it.

Max M. Power

Everyone has a
breaking point.
I have well exceeded
mine.

Max M. Power

I do silly things to make myself laugh. If you laugh too that's just an added bonus.

Max M. Power

With my head hung low I whisper,
"Hello Darkness, my old friend."

"Nothing about this visit will be
pleasant," he replies with a smile,
"for you anyway."

Max M. Power

*I need help. In my head I'm
screaming, but nothing escapes my
lips. If you ask, I'll lie, saying,
"I'm fine."
No, I can not ask for it, if I try I
shut down.
Yes, I need help.
Please. Help.*

Max M. Power

Agape and I have been working hard on the 2nd addition of Let It Be, Speaking Words of Wisdom... Sort of. There are new memes as well as the old ones remade so you can read them easier. Each meme will have an explanation of what I was thinking when I wrote it. I will be posting the new memes here once a day so get ready. Remember, you are not alone and it's okay not to be okay.

Max M. Power

The most deadliest scars are the ones no one can see for they were born of a broken soul.

Max M. Power

Demons love the fire.
They embrace it, crave it,
and long to be near it.
Within the flames they are
truly home.

Max M. Power

Everyone wants to be the hero until they realize they are actually the villain.

Max M. Power

The universe is just an
open door away.

Max M. Power

Live and love in the here and now for no one is promised tomorrow.

Max M. Power

Don't give up the chase for
you are worth the pursuit.

Max M. Power

Grief comes to us all for a variety of reasons, not just Death.

There is no time table on how to grieve.

Max M. Power

Maybe I'm a drain.

Maybe I'm in extreme pain.

Maybe, just maybe,

I'm completely insane!

Max M. Power

No one can hate me worse than myself.

Max M. Power

Silence is often the scariest sound in the universe.

Max M. Power

Never fear your scars.
Embrace them.

Max M. Power

Beauty comes from the soul despite how the wrapping looks.

Max M. Power

Never will you find a more beautiful soul than one that has curves.

Max M. Power

People fear what they themselves do not understand. If someone attacks you, it is because they sense strength and a power they only wish they had. Do not let your light dim for anyone.

Max M. Power

I *am afraid of the silence.*

Max M. Power

Every morning I ask myself what mask shall I wear today?

Max M. Power

Even the mightiest warrior can grow tired of the battle.

Max M. Power

When someone asks if you're okay it's alright to say No.

Max M. Power

The words, "I have depression," should not invoke fear in anyone no more than "I have brown eyes," should, for it is who you are.

Max M. Power

Having a mental affliction is NOT the same as having the common cold.

Max M. Power

Be the reason someone smiles.

Max M. Power

Do you ever feel like you're someone else's play thing?

Max M. Power

I want to die
but monsters never die.

Max M. Power

The kindest soul can become the deadliest monster.

Max M. Power

Sometimes the demons win.

Max M. Power

Lie

The lie I tell myself,
"I am not insane."
A dark laughter soon follows
As my demons pull me close.

"No," I scream
But I can not fight them.
My world grows dark
Frost is in the air.

They hold me tight
There is no escape,
As they whisper in my ear
"You belong to us."

"Finally,
You are one of us,
A devil, a demon,"
Chaos is all that remains.

A dark laughter fills the air
The voice is my own.
The lie, I tell myself,
"I am not insane."

Max M. Power

In Your Head

What do you do,
You can't stay in bed
How do you run from,
What's in your head?
My demons call to me,
I've heard what's been said.
How do you run from
What's in your head?
The dark thoughts
They are easily fed.
How do you run from,
What's in your head?

I've fought
And I've bled.
How do you run from,
What's in your head?
I'm so tired
Thin I've been spread.
How do you run from
What's in your head?
I don't want to lose,
I'm afraid of my deathbed.
Answer me please,
How do you run from,
What's in your head?

Max M. Power

The Monster Within

The monster within
Is clawing to break free.
He's destroying
Everything inside of me.

I don't think I can win,
This time he is too strong.
My light is going out,
My life is gone.

Max M. Power

My demons
I can no longer fight.
I've given up,
Succumbed to the night.

I belong to them,
They are in control.
I have lost.
I have no soul.

Max M. Power

I looked out into the world
At all the loves that
Are meant to be.
I begged the universe for
A love like that,
It replied no such love
Is meant for a monster
Like me.

Max M. Power

I am a healer of broken
souls.
I can heal anyone
except my own soul.

Max M. Power

If you want to fight me because I gave someone a hug, you just want to watch the world burn.

Max M. Power

"Shut up. No one cares."
Those five words can destroy someone
who is trying to share something they are
passionate about. If someone silences
themselves and apologizes for speaking,
they have been destroyed by these words
before.

Max M. Power

Why am I broken and so worthless?

Max M. Power

There's a storm brewing, it's going to be bad.
I can feel it, unlike anything I've ever had.
Nothing you say or do can stop it.
Please bear with me until once again I am fit.

Max M. Power

It only takes a small spark to ignite a mighty blaze.

Max M. Power

Madness

In the darkness
Alone I sit.
Descending into madness
Just for a bit.

I close my eyes
No difference it makes
Soon the madness
Over me it takes.

Cold I feel
As I begin to cry.
It's the madness
Causing my sigh.

I don't want
To be left alone.
I fear the madness
And the places it roams.

Save me
I beg of you.
Don't let the madness
Do what it will do.

Max M. Power

My Civil War

"When you go dark, you really go dark."
"What part of evil don't you understand?"
"But you're so nice every day."
"That's how I hide in plain sight."
"You're just saying that, joking again."
"No, it's what monsters do."
"You are not a monster."
"See, I have you fooled."
"I will hurt you, I will destroy your soul."
"I am true evil, disguised as an angel."
"I don't believe you, I can't."
"Believe what you want but it's who we truly are."
"I am nothing like you."
"You ARE me!"

Max M. Power

One day you shall rise up, everything will go your way, and the world will be yours!

TODAY!

Today is not that day.
Today you hide under the covers and won't come out till tomorrow.
Today... the universe will devour your soul.

Max M. Power

I am here for you
To help weather the storm.
I have tissue
For the tears are sure to fall.
My shoulder is here
To give you a place to lean on.
My arms are open
To keep you safe in my embrace.
I have an ear
Fill it with your words of woe.
I am here
To stand with you in silence
For you are never alone.

Max M. Power

*If you could see my scars
you would look away in horror.
Not one inch of my flesh
would be safe.*

Max M. Power

No one's life has ever been
improved by my being in it.

Max M. Power

Read more books by:

Max M. Power

Let It Be

ABOUT THE AUTHOR

Max was born in a library, surrounded by books from all over the galaxy. His gypsy soul never stayed in one place for very long as he traveled the universe, having many great adventures, all while lying on the carpet floor in his living room.

Max has been writing fiction for over twenty years but is now focusing his efforts on promoting Mental Health Awareness by sharing his personal struggles with others.

His books span from poetry and short stories to general fiction and action adventure novels.

Anxiety, bipolar, and depression may be his diagnosis, but that is not who he is as a person. He hopes to end the negative stigma, one Free Hug at a time.

www.ingramcontent.com/pod-product-compliance
Lightning Source LLC
Chambersburg PA
CBHW061641250726

48659CB00004B/1331